LATINOS
IN THE
LIMELIGHT

WITHDRAWN

Christina Aguilera   John Leguizamo

Antonio Banderas   Jennifer Lopez

Jeff Bezos   Ricky Martin

Oscar De La Hoya   Pedro Martinez

Cameron Diaz   Freddie Prinze Jr.

Scott Gomez   Selena

Salma Hayek   Carlos Santana

Enrique Iglesias   Sammy Sosa

CHELSEA HOUSE PUBLISHERS

LATINOS
IN THE
LIMELIGHT

Carlos Santana

Henna Remstein

CHELSEA HOUSE PUBLISHERS
Philadelphia

Frontis: Carlos Santana has won an enthusiastic global audience with five decades of electrifying performances and nearly three dozen albums.

CHELSEA HOUSE PUBLISHERS

Editor in Chief: Sally Cheney
Director of Production: Kim Shinners
Production Manager: Pamela Loos
Art Director: Sara Davis
Editor: Bill Conn
Production Editor: Diann Grasse

Layout by
21st Century Publishing and Communications, Inc.
http://www.21cpc.com

The Chelsea House World Wide Web address is
http://www.chelseahouse.com

First Printing

1 3 5 7 9 8 6 4 2

CIP applied for ISBN 0-7910-6473-5

CONTENTS

"THE SWEETEST MAN"

Veteran rocker Carlos Santana made history on February 23, 2000 at the 42nd Annual Grammy Awards in Los Angeles, California. Santana had been nominated in 11 categories and walked away with nine awards. Despite competition from younger acts like Backstreet Boys and Britney Spears, 52-year-old Santana was the one who made history by tying Michael Jackson's 1983 record for the most awards won in one evening.

Nine times Santana heard his name announced as a winner. Nine times he stepped to the stage to accept his awards for the album, *Supernatural*, including the most prized Album of the Year Award. Each time he delivered humble thank-you speeches that spoke of the gratitude he has for finding the magic in music. "This is a supreme moment," he said. "This validates all we're trying to do . . . use music to heal the world."

Later that same year, the Latin Academy of Recording Arts and Sciences (LARAS) held the first annual Latin Grammy Awards on September 13, 2000. Again, Carlos Santana's talent was recognized: he won Record of the Year, Best Pop Instrumental Performance, and Best Rock

Carlos Santana makes history by walking away from the 2000 Grammy Awards with nine awards for his album *Supernatural*, tying the record for a single artist set by Michael Jackson in 1983.

Performance by a Duo or Group with Vocal Latin (with the rock group Man from Guadalajara, Mexico). These honors represented a well-earned nod of recognition from his peers in the Latino community.

The LARAS association also works to improve the quality of life and the cultural condition for Latin music and its makers. They offer educational and cultural programs, as well as networking opportunities. LARAS believes in preserving the identity and vitality of the hundreds of regional forms of Latin music found throughout the world, and it fights on behalf of its members to protect artists' rights.

Before the year 2000 ended, Santana took home many more awards. On November 30, 2000, he was voted Man of the Year at the My VHI Music Awards. Winning this award was especially meaningful to Santana because fans, not music industry members, vote for the winners. Then, at the Billboard Awards on December 5 in Las Vegas, Nevada, *Supernatural* received four more top awards.

As a child, Santana had played folksongs for a mere 50 cents a piece on the streets of his native Mexico. Now, the overwhelming honors he was receiving from the music industry were the fulfillment of his life-long dreams. "I keep pinching myself," he said. "Not too many people get a chance at the brass ring twice."

Carlos Santana first entered the music scene in 1966, when he formed the group he named after himself, Santana. Their music combined Latin influences, like salsa and samba, with blues and traditional hardcore rock 'n' roll rhythms. The group's brilliant performance at Woodstock, the legendary

three-day music festival held in 1969 in upstate New York, set a new standard for rock guitar and live performance. Shortly after their trailblazing Woodstock performance, Santana released their first album, *Santana*. The album reached number four on the American charts. A year later, the band's second album, *Abraxas*, made it all the way to number one on the American charts.

Combining salsa and samba with blues and traditional hard rock, Santana's crisp sound and flamboyant licks set a new standard for rock guitar during a sizzling performance at Woodstock in 1969.

Since his first early hits 30 years ago Santana has teamed up with various artists, fusing his trademark guitar sound with jazz, blues, Tex-Mex, and other types of music. However, his early breakout successes seemed to be fading in the 1980s and early 1990s. Even then, however, his rock fans remained loyal to his talent. Rock radio stations continued to play his classic songs like "Black Magic Woman," and his live concerts were always sold out, even at large concert halls like Madison Square Garden in New York City.

Clearly, Santana was no stranger to success, but the careers of many musicians at his age tend to be winding down. After recording 35 solo and group albums in his career, however, *Supernatural* provided a second chance for Santana to prove his stunning talent. More than 30 years after he first achieved fame, his latest album drew a huge, diverse audience. Popular radio stations played the new music relentlessly. All across the world, people— critics, fans, the media, and fellow musicians— were talking about *Supernatural*'s hit songs.

And everyone was buying *Supernatural*, too. As of December 2000, the album had sold over 10 million copies. Santana's faithful rock fans bought the CD, but so did new fans. Fans of Top 40, hip-hop, jazz, and other forms of music, all bought *Supernatural* to hear Santana's innovative guitar playing on unique collaborations with a lineup of top musicians, including Lauryn Hill, Everlast, Dave Matthews, Rob Thomas, Eagle Eye Cherry, Eric Clapton, and Beck and Beastie Boys' producers, the Dust Brothers.

Santana named his album for the "supernatural" combinations of talented singers, musicians, and producers on each of its songs. The creative pairings of artists blended many different musical backgrounds, from Latin rock to Afro-Cuban, from rap to mainstream popular music.

The album was a super-seller that skyrocketed up the record charts. Shortly after

the Grammy Awards, Santana embarked on a world tour, playing for sold-out audiences all over Europe, Japan, Canada, and the United States.

The rebirth of Santana's popularity was also fueled by a song called "Smooth," a collaboration between Santana and Rob Thomas, lead singer of the group Matchbox 20. Thomas wrote the record-breaking song, which was named Song of the Year at the 42nd Annual Grammy Awards, and performed it with Santana live at the ceremony. The enthusiastic audience danced in their seats to its familiar, Latin-infused rhythms. For the members of Matchbox 20, Thomas says playing with Santana "reverted

Teaming with Matchbox 20's Rob Thomas, Santana scores a monster hit with the song *Smooth*. Here Santana and Thomas perform the song at the 2000 Grammy Awards.

[them] back to that 16-year-old kid playing air guitar in front of the mirror." It was hard for them to believe they were recording Thomas' song with an admired rock legend. "Smooth" spent 12 consecutive weeks at number one on *Billboard* magazine's charts.

Santana's new round of success is even sweeter because he has also achieved peace in his personal life. With the support of his wife Deborah and their three children, Santana worked hard in the 1990s to face his difficulties. He overcame drug use and found an inner peace after a lifetime of seeking ever-deeper spirituality. Today, he is devoted to his family and to making music.

When he is not making music, Santana uses his fame to return something to the community. Encouragement from one of his own grade-school teachers taught Santana the power educators have to encourage young people to follow their dreams. That experience fueled Santana's determination to use education to help other children find their own passions in life. He has worked with the National Education Association of the United States to recruit Latino, African American, and other minority teachers. He and his wife also founded the Milagro Foundation, an organization that funds education, medical, and housing needs for children around the world.

As he moves into the 21st century, a more meditative Santana has found his largest audience ever through music that reflects the Latin roots of his birthplace in rural Mexico and his early childhood in the city of Tijuana, where he watched his father work as a mariachi violinist. His commitment to his music, his heritage, and his spiritual values has made him well respected by both fellow musicians and the public. Rock legend and fellow guitarist Eric Clapton, a longtime friend, calls Santana "the sweetest man I know."

But Santana didn't reach where he is today easily. The road from rural Mexico to the Grammy Awards was a long and bumpy one.

2

MEXICO: SANTANA'S FIRST TASTE OF MUSIC

Carlos Santana was the fourth child of José Santana and Josefina Barragan. He was born on July 20, 1947, in Autlán de Navarro, in the state of Jalisco, Mexico, where both of his parents had grown up. The rural town south of Mexico City had few modern conveniences; there were no paved roads, no electricity, and no running water. For the first seven years of Santana's life, he and his six brothers and sisters spent a peaceful, simple childhood there in Autlán. When it rained, Carlos made paper boats and watched them sail down the streets. He watched for his father to come home from work, and he loved to listen to his father's stories. These stories were often about a tiger, and his father would skillfully build the tension as the story progressed; later, as an adult, Santana would apply his understanding of storytelling and suspense to his guitar solos.

Santana's parents, who had married in 1940, ran a traditional and religious household. Santana's grand-father, Antonino, had been a musician who played the French horn in a local band. He had passed on a musical legacy to Santana's father, José, when he taught him to play the violin. As an adult, José worked as a musician,

Santana's exciting rhythms and blistering lead guitar style have earned him a worldwide audience. Here he is performing at the Tabernacle in London.

and he was successful enough that he was able to support his family on his earnings. José did, however, have to move frequently, depending on where he could find work, and so he was often absent from his family.

In his teens, José had played in and later lead a local symphony. By the time he married Josefina, he was bandleader of a group called Los Cardinales. Los Cardinales began playing American swing and jazz songs, like those of Duke Ellington and Cole Porter. In the late 1940s, the band embraced the mariachi—a popular form of music that originated in the state of Jalisco where the Santanas lived. Because Los Cardinales often played at weddings, baptisms, and parties, they were celebrities in their hometown. Friends and neighbors loved dancing to their mariachi-style waltzes and fast-paced tangos

There was a close bond between all the Santana children and their parents, but Carlos found a special connection with his father. Very early in life, Santana fell in love with music. The sounds, the dancing, and the costumes of traveling mariachi bands entranced him as a small child. He loved to watch his father's performance: for him, it was a powerful and magical experience.

When Santana was five years old, José began teaching his middle son how to play the violin. Over the next seven years, Santana learned the fundamentals of music from those violin lessons. He never excelled at the violin, but through those lessons he learned something much more valuable from his father: being a musician was a true and noble profession.

When Santana turned seven, his father traveled with Los Cardinales to Tijuana, Mexico. A

Carlos Santana was born in Autlán de Navarro, a rural Mexican town with no paved roads, no electricity, and no running water. In 2001 Santana's hometown honored his achievements by presenting him with the key to the city.

year later, the rest of the family joined him. Carlos, his brothers Antonio and Jorge, and his sisters Laura, Irma, Leticia, and Maria spent the next six years in the northern Mexico town on the border of the United States.

Compared to Autlán, Tijuana was crowded and filled with cheap bars catering to tourists. The Santanas first lived in a half-built hotel without furniture, doors, or windows. To help earn money for the family, Santana played Mexican folk music for tourists for 50 cents a song, and he and his older brother sold Chiclets gum and shined shoes. Luckily, this situation was only temporary. A few months later they moved to a somewhat better neighborhood where Santana went to Catholic school and played sports. At church, he played with the orchestra. He began to teach himself English by watching television through their neighbors' open doors.

Music remained a constant in his life. In addition to his father's traditional mariachi music, Santana now heard music from the United States on the radio. His parents also regularly played classical music at home—Mozart, Beethoven, and Brahms. José Santana had hopes that his son would follow in his footsteps, so Santana studied at a local music college after regular school hours for a short time. He and his father often played together at home, and at the age of 10, Santana joined his father's band on the streets and in the bars of Tijuana.

In those bars, young Santana grew up quickly. Dangerous criminals, prostitutes, and drunken tourists were the usual audience. He saw plenty of knife fights and brawls, and he witnessed many incidents of violence against women. On many nights, tourists requested that the band play the same song over and over again; Santana hated that his father had no control over his own music. Despite the unappealing surroundings, Santana's father had no choice but to play in those places to earn money for the family. Eventually, a frustrated Santana stopped playing with his father; he turned instead to studying American music.

Hours of listening to the radio introduced Santana to a type of American music called the blues. The music he heard was the classic

blues of artists like Muddy Waters, B.B. King, Jimmy Reed, and John Lee Hooker. One night, Santana's mother saw the chance to encourage her son's interest in music by taking him to see a band called the TJs. Santana became an instant fan of the TJs' American-style blues, and he traveled to hear the TJs wherever they played. He especially admired the TJs' guitarist, Javier Batiz. At each show, he would study Batiz's movements; later, he would say that Batiz "dressed like Little Richard, played like B.B. King, with a little Ray Charles thrown in there." For Santana, hearing Batiz's music was like "watching a flying saucer for the first time." Soon he decided he wanted to play like his guitar hero.

Santana's appearance on veteran bluesman John Lee Hooker's albums *Mr. Lucky* and *The Healer* earned critical acclaim and a broader audience for both artists.

In 1960, José Santana traveled across the United States border to San Francisco, California, in search of work. Though separated from his family, José received regular reports of the children's health and activities in his wife's letters. She described Carlos's renewed interest in music. Thrilled to read the news, José sent home a used electric guitar.

Santana quickly taught himself to play the Gibson L5 guitar. His years of violin training easily translated to the new instrument. When he was 12, he landed his first professional job with a local five-piece band, the Strangers. He played with them for several months before moving on to another band called El Convey.

Playing with El Convey forced Santana back into Tijuana's sleazy strip bars. His mother knew this meant her underage son would be in places where women danced naked for men and the police were often called to break up fights. She was unhappy about Santana spending so much time in these bars—but she could not deny Santana the chance to play his music. She ignored her worries and allowed him to continue. He worked seven nights a week, from four in the afternoon until midnight on weeknights, and until six in the morning on the weekends. He earned nine dollars a week.

Since the birth of her first child, Josefina dreamed of raising her children in the United States. In 1962, she decided it was time to leave Tijuana. She filed for immigration papers to move to San Francisco, California, where her husband had been living for the past year. He was working steadily and making a good living to support the family.

Carlos was unhappy about the move. In Mexico, he had a steady gig, friends, and money. In San Francisco, though, he was expected to go back to being a kid. He had nothing in common with the other students at the junior high school; in his own mind, he was an adult. He became more and more frustrated and resentful.

The final straw came when his mother spent the money he had been saving to buy a guitar. He had earned the money that paid for them to travel to San Francisco and for the dental work his sister needed. With the money left over, he had been planning to buy a Stratocaster, a type of electric guitar. When he found the guitar he wanted, he asked his mother for his money—and found that she had used it for food and rent. Carlos sulked for two weeks. Eventually, his mother threw up her hands in exasperation and gave him 20 dollars to return to Tijuana on his own.

Without family support, however, life was difficult. He had to take care of himself like an adult. He barely earned enough money playing guitar to survive, yet he relished his independence. If things had been left up to him, he would have continued to make it on his own—but after a year, his mother and older brother came to get him. Carlos kicked and struggled, but his brother picked him up and threw him in the car. Carlos reluctantly rejoined the family in California, but he would never be a kid again.

3

THE FIRST
SANTANA BAND

In San Francisco, the family settled in the Mission District; the seven kids shared two bedrooms. Santana learned English and attended James Lick Junior High School. After a year on his own, Santana fit in even less with the other kids. To him, they seemed juvenile and silly, and he had little in common with them. After all, his idea of a good time was to hang around with older musicians, talking about Ray Charles and the blues; his fellow students were only interested in playing hooky, stealing cars, and listening to the Beach Boys.

Santana was bored by his classes as well, and he spent his time daydreaming about one day performing with B.B. King. He only did well in one subject—art. He briefly considered studying art in college, but his focus on music won out. He was determined to become a great guitar player.

He finally got his electric guitar—a Gibson Les Paul Junior—only to have his brother's friend sit on it and break it in two. After that incident, the tensions grew between the two brothers, finally ending one night in a scuffle where Santana gave his brother a black eye. When they finally went to bed, Santana spent the night lying on

Santana's unique playing style and high-energy stage show quickly won the band an international following.

the very edge of the bed he shared with his brother, hardly daring to breathe for fear his brother would hit him back. The next day, though, when Santana came home from school, he found waiting for him a brand new white Gibson Les Paul guitar and an amplifier. Santana had to make the payments, but his brother had made the down payment.

Now that he had his own guitar, he met musicians his own age and formed his first band with friends Dan Haro and Gus Rodriguez. Like his father with his band Los Cardinales, Santana's band played at parties, bar mitzvahs, and weddings. Their repertoire included popular songs like James Brown's "Papa's Got a Brand New Bag." At the same time, Santana experimented with new sounds like funk and soul. He hooked up with soul singer Joyce Dunn, who would later become a member of the band Sly and the Family Stone. Together they entered a "battle of the bands" contest sponsored by a local radio station. They did not win, but playing in front of the contest's large audience was a thrill for Santana. The success of his band convinced Santana that he would be able to make a living with music, and he moved out of his parents' home.

During these years, young people across the country were challenging the political and social norms of their parents. Students were protesting the Vietnam War, President John F. Kennedy's assassination in 1963 had left the country shaken, and many young people called "hippies" were rebelling against the "establishment." Hippies were creating and embracing alternative music and lifestyles.

The intersection of two now famous streets in San Francisco, Haight and Ashbury, became the center of the hippie lifestyle. Many legendary bands of the 1960s got their start in the Haight-Ashbury neighborhood. Some of the most famous bands from the era are the Grateful Dead, Jefferson Airplane, Cream, and the Jimi Hendrix Experience.

Santana moved into his own apartment in the Haight-Ashbury area. He loved the care-free hippie attitude toward life. The lifestyle, however, included drugs and drinking, and Santana became convinced that psychedelic drugs like LSD and mescaline helped him make spiritual journeys. He looked at them as the means to learn more about himself, and he plunged into the drug scene. For the next several decades he used drugs heavily.

Working as a dishwasher at the Tic Tock diner, Santana earned money to give his mother. He used whatever money was left over to buy as many record albums as he could. He bought new records every week and listened over and over again to his favorites—Jimmy Reed, B.B. King, John Coltrane, Miles Davis, and the Butterfield Blues Band. He studied them, absorbed them, learned the sounds, and then interpreted those sounds to make them his own.

At the Fillmore West, a local club where many rock, jazz, and blues legends got started in the 1960s, he and his friends saw many live performances by musicians such as Junior Wells, John Lee Hooker, Joe Henderson, Elvin Jones, Bola Sete, Otis Redding, Eric Clapton, and many other up-and-coming musicians. After months of admiring other musicians on stage, Santana walked into the Fillmore one night and was given the opportunity of a life-time. The guitarist from the headlining act of Butterfield Blues Band failed to show up—and Santana stepped into his place on stage.

"Wow!" was the dazzled reaction of several important people in the club that night. Santana's impromptu jam became the catalyst that launched him to superstardom.

One of those people at the Fillmore that night was Bill Graham, a big concert promoter who ran the Fillmore West. When he saw Santana play, he immediately asked if he had his own band. Graham already promoted popular '60s bands like the Grateful Dead, Cream, and Janis Joplin with Big Brother and the Holding Company. Santana did not want to lose the chance to play again for Graham, so he said yes, he had a band. Quickly, he put a real band together—the Santana Blues Band.

On drums and bass were old bandmates Danny Haro and Gus Rodriguez. Gregg Rolie was on keyboard, new friend Tom Frazier joined in, and Mike Carabello was on drums. And, of course, Carlos Santana sang and played guitar. The band practiced in a garage, and they mixed imagination and improvisation with their renditions of popular songs. They jammed in parks or on the street just to be able to see people react to their music while they made pocket change. After such impromptu jams for passers-by, the Santana Blues Band played to their largest audience at an early performance at a "Be-In" in Golden Gate Park. The crowd's reaction was a thrill, and Carlos Santana wanted more.

The addition of a Latin conga beat to Santana's songs made them very different from other rock bands playing around San Francisco. Audiences noticed the difference, and the band's popularity grew. By January of 1967, they were playing the Sunday afternoon slot at the Fillmore. Soon after, Bill Graham invited them to open for bands like

Bill Graham has been one of Santana's strongest supporters. When Graham heard of a big rock festival to take place at Woodstock in 1969, he offered to help book the headline bands, provided that Santana be included in the lineup. Here Graham joins Santana at the Bay Area Music Awards in 1981.

Sly and the Family Stone and Creedence Clearwater Revival.

In the midst of this budding success, Carlos Santana received bad news that brought it all to a temporary halt. The band had just opened for the British rock group the Who when Santana was diagnosed with tuberculosis, a disease affecting his lungs. He ended up spending three months in the hospital.

A tutor visited him since he still had not graduated from high school, and he did eventually graduate while he was in the hospital. Santana was restless, though, with nothing to do except watch television. He looked forward to visits from his friends. Many of them brought him drugs to "cheer him up." When Santana could no longer stand the boredom of the hospital, he left without his doctor's permission.

During his hospital stay, the Santana Blues Band had fallen apart. When he finally returned to the music scene, his roommate Stan Marcum recruited drummer Bob "Doc" Livingston and bassist David Brown. They decided to drop the "Blues Band" in their name and became simply "Santana."

The band members lived and breathed music, and their new band drew a big following. They played as many shows as they could in 1967 and 1968, leaping at any chance to perform in front of a live audience. Unlike many bands, Santana would play any club at any time; they were known for filling in for other bands that at the last minute did not show up. Their constant performing paid off when promoter Bill Graham booked Santana as the headline act at the Fillmore for June 16, 1968.

In the two years since Carlos had moved out of his family home, he had lost touch with his parents. He had not wanted them to see him as a failure. But with the success of his band, Carlos decided to call his parents and invite them to see his big show at the Fillmore. They were thrilled to hear from their son. Though they were shocked by the hippie culture they encountered at the show, they were proud of their son's accomplishment.

Other successful bands like Chicago and Steppenwolf began booking Santana to play as their opening act. This exposure gave Santana

In the group's early days, Santana seized any chance to perform for a live audience. Unlike many bands, Santana would play any club at any time. In 1968, around the time of this early publicity photo, the group signed a contract with Columbia Records.

confidence and still more fans. In September 1968, Santana played alongside well-known bands like the Grateful Dead, Muddy Waters, and Country Joe and the Fish in front of the largest crowd to date at the Sky River Rock Festival and the Lighter Than Air Fair. Record companies were signing these and other bands that were emerging out of the San Francisco psychedelic music scene, and they soon took notice of Santana's growing popularity.

Several record labels pursued the band, but Santana eventually signed with Columbia. The band was at its best in front of a live audience, however, and none of the band members had ever been in a recording studio before. To make matters worse, the record company was not happy with the songs they wrote for their first album.

Carlos Santana and his friends again reorganized the band. Drummer Doc Livingston was replaced with a new percussionist named José "Chepito" Areas, an experienced drummer who could play bongos and timbales. José "Chepita" Areas was born in Nicaragua, and was given the nickname "Chepita" because of his small size. (In Spanish, "Chepita" means "chipmunk.") He showed musical talent early in childhood and grew up to become a skilled musician and an expert in Latin music. Areas introduced the other Santana band members to Latin rhythms like the cha-cha and the merengue (a rhythm that originated in the Dominican Republic). He also used his bongo and timbales to contribute the Latin sound to Santana's music. (Bongos are small drums that are played with the fingers. Timbales are another type of drum fitted with tight skins that produce a high-pitched tone.) This Santana line-up finally produced their debut album, called *Santana*, which was released in October 1969.

On *Santana*, songs like "Evil Ways," "Savor," and "Shades of Time" featured a tighter sound than Santana's signature on-stage improvisations. The Latin flavor of the rock album was completely new to audiences. It combined the intense guitar playing of Carlos Santana, the rhythms of three drummers (including the thunderous percussion of new member Areas), and compelling bass tracks. Many of these songs are still favorites of classic rock radio. The extraordinary album earned Santana double-platinum status.

In December the same year, Santana played

a series of four headline shows at the Fillmore West. The shows gave David Rubinstein, a young record producer from Columbia Records, a great idea to record the live performances. At the time, Rubinstein used the recordings to give the band ideas for their studio recordings. In 1997, nearly 30 years later, these concert recordings were released as a two-CD set called *Live at the Fillmore '68*. The music on these CDs is an interesting window on Santana's early days, and many fans saw it as a fitting tribute to Carlos Santana's career.

But back in 1968, Carlos still had no idea how far his career would go. His biggest break was yet to come.

Drummer and percussionist José "Chepito" Areas joined the Santana line-up in 1969, in time to appear on the group's debut album, *Santana*. After suffering a brain aneurysm in 1971, Areas was forced to leave the band before the recording of *Santana III*.

WOODSTOCK BRINGS
SANTANA TO THE MASSES

By 1969, Bill Graham had become one of Santana's strongest supporters. When Graham heard of a big rock festival taking place in mid-August in a rural area of Sullivan County, New York, he contacted the concert promoters. He discovered they were having trouble signing up some of the bigger name bands that Graham happened to represent. Graham offered to help get the headline bands on board, with the provision that the concert promoters also include Santana in the lineup. They agreed.

Santana had been gaining a larger audience but still was not well known outside of California. Woodstock Music and Art Fair would provide an opportunity to bring the group's music to a national audience.

The slogan for the event read "a three-day festival of peace and music." Held on August 15, 16, and 17, 1969, Woodstock has become a rock music legend. Though ads for the "world's biggest rock concert" ran in newspapers and on radio in major cities on the East and West Coast—from New York and Boston, to San Francisco and Los Angeles—its organizers underestimated Woodstock's appeal. They expected 60,000 people to attend.

Santana performed at Woodstock on August 16, 1969. When the concert film was released in theaters, the group gained national celebrity.

Nearly half a million people showed up.

Hundreds of thousands of teenagers and college students poured into the area. Traffic jams blocked the two-lane roads for miles around the site in the remote farming community. Police were forced to close the New York State Thruway.

When the crowds finally made their way to the concert site, they overwhelmed the ticket gates and hopped the flimsy fences. Thousands entered free. This put the concert promoters several million dollars in debt, but the flow of people could not be controlled. At this point, the promoters' main concern turned to the crowd's safety and enjoyment. They unanimously agreed to announce that Woodstock had officially become a free concert.

Concert-goers camped on miles of surrounding hog farms. The weather did not cooperate; after driving rain and thunderstorms, Woodstock turned into a sea of mud and people that public officials eventually declared a disaster area. Regardless of the conditions, fans inside the festival grounds enjoyed band after band from morning to night.

The Grateful Dead, Jimi Hendrix, Janis Joplin, Sly and the Family Stone, Jefferson Airplane, Richie Havens, Joan Baez, and Crosby, Stills, Nash & Young, among many others, gave stunning performances. Listening to each act, the audience seemed to react and move as one organism.

On Saturday, August 16, Santana flew by helicopter to Woodstock. The band took their positions on stage in the early afternoon, where they played for over an hour with all their hearts and souls. The music was explosive and kept the audience entranced.

A film of the entire event reveals why Woodstock has been hailed as a turning point for many of the rock musicians who played there. The rock documentary also shows the masses of people and their carefree attitude, both of which helped create the Woodstock mystique that has become part of American social history.

When the Woodstock film was released in movie theaters, Santana and other Woodstock performers became recognizable celebrities. Soon after playing Woodstock, the album *Santana* reached number four on the *Billboard* charts. Record companies realized the appeal of this new music and began heavily promoting Santana and the other 1960s rock bands that were the driving phenomenon behind psychedelic rock.

Two subsequent Woodstock festivals have tried to capture the original spirit of the legendary 1969 concert. In 1994, 30 acts performed at Woodstock '94 from August 12 to 14 in

Held on August 15-17, 1969, Woodstock has become a rock music legend. A concert that drew nearly a half million fans, Woodstock was billed as "a three-day festival of peace and music" and proved to be a breakthrough appearance for Santana.

Saugerties, New York. Santana was among them. On the 30-year anniversary of Woodstock, promoters scheduled another attempt to repeat history from July 23-25 in Rome, New York. At Woodstock '99 the number of fans reached 250,000. However, the 1999 Woodstock ended with a frightening fire and a small riot. Woodstocks '94 and '99 showcased popular bands of the time, but the spontaneity and uniqueness could not be recaptured.

On December 6th, 1969, Santana played alongside the British band the Rolling Stones at another large, free show at the Altamont Racetrack in San Francisco. Unlike the peaceful Woodstock event, the Altamont show turned violent. Members of the Hells Angels motorcycle gang had been hired as security, and they reportedly tried to control the concert's chaos by striking back violently.

As Santana played, people in the audience near the stage battled with the Hells Angels. Fights broke out in the crowd. The mayhem ended in one teenager being killed in front of the stage. The brawls reminded Santana of his early adolescence in the bars of Tijuana; he was sickened by what he saw. Some music historians have said the hippie era of love and peace ended that day at the Altamont Racetrack.

It was a tragic and badly planned event—and yet the music it celebrated continued to capture the hearts of fans, as did Santana. Throughout 1970, Santana toured the United States, playing continuously to support the band's hot selling album, Santana. To promote Santana's overseas release, the band toured Europe for the first time, playing to sold-out crowds. Two highlights of their European tour included performances at Royal Albert Hall in

London, England, and at the Montreaux Jazz Festival in Switzerland.

The band was continuing to develop their music. Their new album, *Abraxas*, had tracks that added variety, such as the fresh sounds from organist Gregg Rolie and the Spanish lyrics sung by Rico Reyes, a singer the band knew from the Haight-Ashbury neighborhood. Lengthy instrumental breaks with no vocals gave the album an air of sophistication, and reworked versions of older Santana material produced three songs that have become synonymous with Santana: "Black Magic Woman," "Gypsy Queen," and "Oye Como Va."

Many fans and critics agree that *Abraxas* is Santana's finest album. *Rock: Rough Guides* says "the musicianship is faultless, with a mix that allows every member to shine."

But although the band had achieved professional success, personally and emotionally they were about to hit some rough roads.

Santana's mix of Latin rhythms and rock guitar has proven as popular in Europe as in the United States. Here they are on stage in London.

THE END OF
THE SANTANA BAND

*A*braxas stayed on the Billboard charts for over a year and half, reaching its peak at number one for six weeks. The album did equally well in Europe, and wealth and fame rained down on Santana band members. After *Abraxas*, the band took some time off. Carlos Santana rehearsed with other musicians, but he had no immediate plans for recording or more touring.

Meanwhile, LSD and cocaine were becoming a more and more frequent part of Carlos Santana's life—and his playing and career choices were beginning to be affected. Using psychedelic drugs, Santana told *Rolling Stone* magazine, was "a spiritual thing, you know. . . . It made me aware of splendor and rapture."

On one occasion, Santana and the band's new young guitar player Neal Schon had the opportunity to jam with British blues guitarist Eric Clapton. That day, Santana was under the influence of LSD and was too incapacitated to join an impromptu jam session. Schon impressed Clapton so much that the next day Clapton offered the teenager a job with his band, Derek and the Dominos. Santana had to act quickly to keep Schon in his own band. The incident

---

Released in 1970, the group's album *Abraxas* included songs that have become synonymous with Santana: "Black Magic Woman," "Gypsy Queen," and "Oye Como Va."

enraged the other Santana band members, and the once close-knit band began to grow apart.

The pressure of living up to their record company's expectations took its toll on the group, too. Promoters were booking Santana to perform constantly, sometimes at a moment's notice. The band had no choice but to comply.

In February 1971, Santana drummer Chepito Areas suffered an aneurysm in his brain. The burst vessel nearly killed him. Areas had been a guiding force in the Santana band and fellow drummer Michael Carabello did not want to play without him. Despite Carabello's reservations, the Santana band did play a major concert in Ghana, Africa, with fellow American singers, Roberta Flack, Wilson Picket, and Tina Turner. They also embarked on a second European tour with a series of replacement percussionists who filled in for Areas. But while they were in Europe, tensions continued to mount between the band members. Carlos Santana himself was confused and discontent.

Putting their problems aside, however, the Santana band returned to California to work on their next album, *Santana III*. The band recorded their third album through the summer of 1971, hoping to match the phenomenal success of *Abraxas*. Coke Escovedo, a percussionist who had joined the band for its European tour, recorded with the band.

Meanwhile, though, Carlos Santana continued to drift away from the other band members, both personally and musically. One of the reasons for his gradual withdrawal was the rock 'n' roll lifestyle that the band participated in together. Santana was still using psychedelic drugs, but he had stopped taking cocaine, while the other band members were using cocaine and heroin. Carlos worried that their heavy drug use would eventually interfere with their ability to perform; he had nightmares that one night they would be performing in front of an audience of 60,000 people and simply fall over, too high on drugs to play.

Carlos was also becoming more introspective. His musical interests at the time were moving in a different direction from those of the other members of the band. While they mostly preferred hardcore rock, Santana was becoming intrigued by jazz music created by artists like Weather Report and Miles Davis.

Despite their disagreements, the band members managed to work together to produce a critically praised album. The album fused their quintessential Latin, rock, blues, jazz, and instrumental sounds that had made the prior two albums hits. *Santana III* spent five weeks on the *Billboard* charts and received favorable reviews from music critics. The band was so exhausted, though, that they hardly enjoyed the new album's success.

Though the band continued to be at odds with each other, they all agreed to play on the closing night of the Fillmore West. Bill Graham asked Santana to be the final act on the club's last night of business, July 4, 1971. The band's tight, passionate performance that night showed no signs of their troubles. They played in tribute to the club and to the man who had helped launch their band and many others in the 1960s rock era.

Next on the agenda for the band was a U.S. tour. Carlos Santana had been spending most of his time recording with Latin trumpeter Luis Casca for his album *For Those Who Chant*. Before the tour, Santana did not see or

Santana's music reflects the Latin roots of his birthplace in rural Mexico and his early childhood in the city of Tijuana, where he watched his father work as a mariachi violinist.

rehearse with his own band for months.

The tour started in the fall, but Carlos Santana did not join the band for the first three shows. Then drummer Michael Carabello quit. The band barely made it through the remaining dates of the short-lived tour. Their minimal efforts did little to promote *Santana III*.

On December 11, 1971, the Santana band, with several stand-ins for departed members, played an ill-fated show in Lima, Peru. For reasons still unknown, the crowd in Lima turned violent.

The government deported the band and confiscated $400,000 worth of equipment. For Carlos Santana, the incident underscored the band's problems, and he officially took back his name from the group, sending the band members their separate ways. Carlos ended the year feeling exhausted and uncertain about his musical future.

Although many members of the band were angry with Carlos, signs had been pointing to the band's demise for nearly a year. "I think it's what happens in most bands," Carlos said reflectively. "If you've played out everything you can play with that particular band, you need to let those people go so you can grow musically and spiritually."

Carlos was ready to grow.

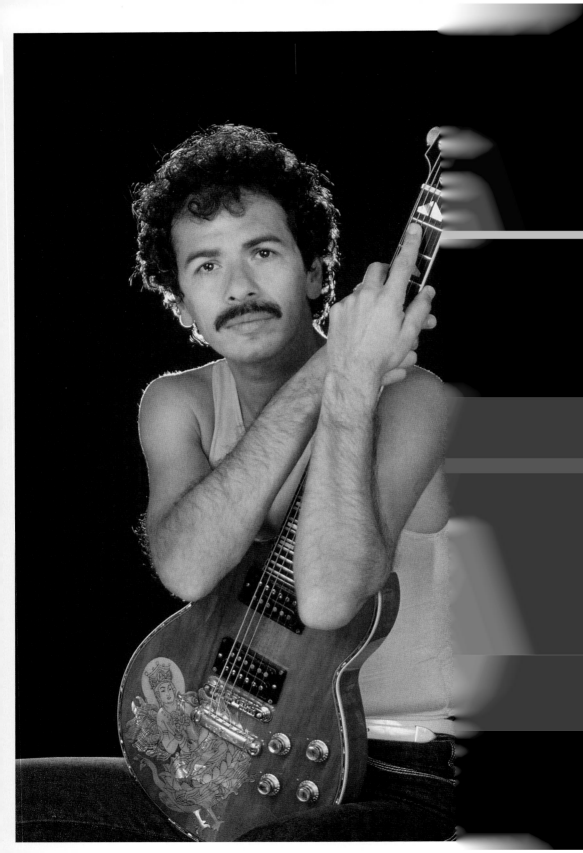

6

THE MUSICAL AND
SPIRITUAL JOURNEY

Santana began looking inward for clarity and enlightenment, the beginning of a lifelong journey. He started reading philosophy and spiritual teachings. He learned meditation. He began fasting and praying while he studied Eastern mysticism. He found it very different from the Catholicism of his childhood.

In 1972, English guitar player John McLaughlin introduced Santana to Indian spiritual guru Sri Chinmoy. The spiritual teacher seemed to embody the peace that Santana had been searching for, and Santana became a practitioner of Chinmoy's teachings. Chinmoy gave his new disciple the name Davadip, which means "the eye, the lamp of the light of God."

Santana cut off his long hair, became a vegetarian, started long-distance running, and totally gave up drugs. It proved an easy transformation: "I never wanted to be a casualty. I didn't want to be a loser. For a long time I was afraid that I wasn't strong enough to shake off the booze and drugs. But with Sri Chinmoy I saw a very simple clarity."

McLaughlin and Santana shared their spiritual quest through music. In 1973, the two guitarists recorded an album

---

After struggling for years with drugs and alcohol, Santana met guru Sri Chimnoy in 1972, who helped him follow a more spiritual path. Santana became a vegetarian, started long-distance running, and gave up drugs. "I never wanted to be a casualty," Santana later said.

together that was a tribute to Sri Chinmoy and his Mahavishnu Orchestra. *Love Devotion Surrender* was a creative departure from Santana's earlier recordings. Santana found the process inspiring, and quickly focused this newfound energy on his next album, *Welcome*. The album did not produce a hit single, but it sold well among Santana fans, reaching number 25 on the *Billboard* charts.

The same year, Santana met his future wife at a Tower of Power concert. He was drawn to her instantly. The friend he was with noticed the way he was looking at her across the room. "It's all over for you, man," the friend told him. "That's the one."

From her side of the room, Deborah King noticed him as well. She didn't recognize him, though, and she had to ask someone who the skinny guy with the guitar was.

Deborah was 22 and ran a vegetarian restaurant in San Francisco, and the couple soon discovered they had much in common. She also ran marathons, and they shared a common quest for personal enlightenment and an interest in Eastern spiritual values. Religious exploration and devotion marked their early relationship. The couple also shared a love of music; Deborah was the daughter of Saunders King, a blues musician, so they both came from musical backgrounds. With so much to draw them together, they fell in love quickly. In the midst of a world tour, Carlos and Deborah were married on April 20, 1973.

Earlier, however, in June 1972, Carlos realized he had ties to his former band and a recording contract to honor. He formed a new studio band with two former Santana members: drummer Gregg Rolie and guitarist/keyboardist Neal Schon. Schon and Rolie had already joined the band *Journey*, but they made time to work with Santana. With a handful of other studio musicians, they produced the album *Caravanserai*, which was released in November 1972.

Caravanserai departed from the Latin rock sound. Instead, Santana produced jazz-inspired, meditative songs. Columbia President Clive Davis was unhappy with the new direction and did not believe radio stations would play the album. Davis's fears proved to be justified to some extent: *Caravanserai* did not produce a hit single. Despite that, however, Santana fans were loyal and bought enough albums for it to reach number eight on the record charts. Compared to the runaway sales of previous albums, however, *Caravanserai* was not a commercial success.

In 1973, Santana married Deborah King, the daughter of a blues musician, with whom he has three children. Here Deborah joins Carlos as he is inducted into the Rock 'n' Roll Hall of fame in 1998.

Santana toured again, this time with a new lineup of musicians. They mainly played new music from *Caravanserai*, and some fans were disappointed. Despite criticism from their fans, they continued to fill concert venues, while their music brought them good reviews from the critics.

Throughout this period in his life, Carlos Santana searched for greater musical inspiration. He played on many other artists' albums, and he teamed up with drummer Buddy Miles. Their jam sessions produced a solid funk and soul album. He also began listening to more jazz artists like Miles Davis, Pharoah Sanders, John Coltrane, Leon Thomas, and others. Soul/jazz vocalist

Leon Thomas booked Santana to join him on tour. Santana was thrilled to perform with this major figure of the New York City jazz scene.

Over the next six years, Santana's life became somewhat predictable. His touring featured mostly new instrumental and jazz-influenced music. Each performance opened with a prayer and moment of meditation. He produced an album per year with Santana Band to appease the record company, often working concurrently on solo projects more in tune with his true musical vision and spiritual interests.

During the late '70s, only the repackaged *Santana's Greatest Hits* album had mass appeal and raced up the Top Twenty *Billboard* Chart. For the sheer love of performing, Santana played regularly with fellow '60s acts like the Grateful Dead and Bob Dylan at rock shows around the United States.

Santana had always been charitable and interested in doing good works through his music. He now made himself available to play benefit concerts whenever friends asked—from a benefit in support of Rubin "Hurricane" Carter, in jail for a crime he did not commit, to a benefit in support of prisoners' rights at Soledad Prison in California.

In 1975, Bill Graham became Santana's manager. Graham helped with the financial and managerial side of the music business, handling the money and contracts, and booking tours. Graham also offered Santana advice on marketing albums and choosing producers who could balance Santana's intense, spiritual approach to making music.

Graham convinced Santana to work with producer David Rubinstein on his next album, *Amigos*, in an attempt to develop Top 40 songs

that would appeal to popular radio listeners. Santana was looking for meaning in his music, however, and the pop sound of *Amigos* did not have it; working on the album felt hollow to him. Although the experience left him disappointed, *Amigos'* sales were respectable and pleased the record company.

In 1981, Carlos Santana parted from his guru, Sri Chinmoy. Although he had become disillusioned with Chinmoy, Santana felt he took much good from the years he had observed the guru's teachings. "My time with Sri Chinmoy gave me some discipline and an awareness of Eastern philosophy," he said. "But after a while, I began to look at it like my old tennis shoes from Mission High School that didn't fit me anymore."

Soon after he left Chinmoy, he and Deborah had their first child, Salvador. The same year was good for him in other ways as well; his new album *Zebop!* was a success, and its single "Winning" reached the Top Twenty on the *Billboard* charts.

Santana has always been interested in doing good works through his music, frequently playing benefit concerts when asked—from a benefit in support of Rubin "Hurricane" Carter, in jail for a crime he did not commit, to a benefit in support of prisoners' rights at Soledad Prison in California.

The stage was always a place where Santana felt at home, honing his musical talents and trying out new material for the pleasure of a live audience.

Zebop! was a lively, danceable album, and critics called it a commercial comeback. But as Carlos Santana continued to record through the 1980s, he seemed to lose his focus musically. Reviewers panned many of his subsequent releases as uninspired. His next album, *Shinju*, only reached number 22 on the charts.

In 1983, he signed a new contract with Columbia Studies and continued to record albums throughout the 1980s. Unfortunately, his solo all-instrumental *Blues for Salvador* was played only on New Age and jazz radio stations. A commercial flop, *Blues for Salvador* further strained the relationship between Santana and his record company. Columbia was unhappy with the music Santana was creating in the studio and did little to promote his next album, *Viva Santana*. It only reached number 142 on the record charts.

Despite the birth of another child, his daughter Stella, Carlos was struggling, directionless, and angry. The deaths of close friends Miles Davis, Bill Graham, and Stevie Ray Vaughn devastated him. In retrospect, he told *Rolling Stone* magazine that the songs he produced during that time were "so-called career suicides."

One high point in the 1980s, however, was a tour with singer and songwriter Bob Dylan. The tour invigorated Santana. He learned a few new musical tricks and visited countries he had never been to before.

The 20th anniversary of the Santana Blues Band came in 1986, but in contrast to his early rock career, the year was a quiet one for Santana. He toured little and stayed close to home. Although he produced little of his own original work, he did work on other artists' albums, including an album by Aretha Franklin and his idol, John Lee Hooker. He also jumped at the chance to work with Willie Dixon and Los Lobos on a song for the movie *La Bamba*, about the life of 1950s singer Richie Valens. However, his studio failures continued to haunt him.

In 1987, on a tour to support the album *Freedom*, Carlos Santana united with Javier Batiz, the former TJs' guitarist who first inspired Santana as a teen in Tijuana. This tour brought the band to Moscow, where the crowd of 25,000 fans adored Santana. As they traveled through places like Hungary, Israel, Budapest, Paris, and Berlin, each stop brought more cheering fans. Carlos was reminded that music brings people together—and he also realized he still had the commercial appeal to bring out thousands.

The following year, original Santana members reunited for several U.S. concerts. And in 1989, Carlos Santana won the Grammy for Best Rock Instrumental Performance for his *Blues for Salvador* album. With a new decade around the corner, Santana was still enjoying his fame. He still generated creative energy. Music still inspired him.

But somehow that wasn't enough.

A MASTERPIECE
OF JOY

The joy of welcoming his third child, Angelica, in 1990, did not diminish Santana's feelings of depression and self-doubt as his professional career continued on a downward slide. His latest album, *Spirits Dancing in the Flesh*, failed to appeal to fans or radio stations. It barely reached number 85 on the *Billboard* charts. Meanwhile, though, Santana performed live to rave reviews; he decided it was time to find another record company.

In June 1992, Santana signed a multi-album deal with Polydor/PLG Records. He had several offers, but Polydor was the only one that offered him complete creative control. The deal also included the formation of his own record label, Guts & Grace. He soon began work on his first album with Polydor, *Milagro*.

The album was a moderate success that received mixed reviews from critics. One positive review came from *Billboard* magazine, which called the album a "potent, fiery blend, with sweet soulfulness and plenty of extended instrumental passages over the vibrant Latin pulse Santana is known for. It is an exhilarating debut."

However, his next two albums, *Sacred Fire* and *Brothers*,

Santana's record-setting album *Supernatural*, released in 2000, vaulted Santana to the top of the charts again, reaching a new generation of listeners and proving his staying power as a world-class musician.

were again disappointments. Santana had come to a crossroads. He was depressed and unsure about future studio work.

His wife, Deborah, pushed Santana to get professional help and he entered therapy. The psychological counseling helped him deal with events and issues from his childhood, including a history of molestation he had never before talked about.

The therapy helped. He told *Rolling Stone* magazine that he is now "comfortable in my own skin. . . . I am more content with Carlos, and I am more proud of Santana." He was healing emotionally, regaining his strength and spirit.

In 1994, his spiritual life took a new turn when he believed he began receiving messages from an angel called Metatron, whose guidance added to Santana's sense of calm. "I know it sounds really crazy to a lot of people," Santana admitted to *Rolling Stone* magazine, "but it's OK, because I'm not afraid of what people think."

From his belief in angelic guidance, Santana drew a new sense of his personal mission in life. His sense of mission brought him peace at all levels of his life, both personally and professionally. His new confidence gave his music renewed force.

During the mid-1990s, a new influence began to take the spotlight in popular music. Latin singers like Ricky Martin, Marc Anthony, and Jennifer Lopez had brought Latin-influenced music to a mainstream audience. The music industry, radio stations, and fans embraced them. Sales were astounding and the media could not get enough the hot new stars.

This new trend collided with the public's taste for nostalgia. In January 1998, Santana was inducted into the Rock 'n' Roll Hall of Fame.

The same year, Santana's first two hit albums were re-released, *Santana* and *Abraxas*. He also recorded guitar for young soul diva Lauryn Hill's album *Miseducation of Lauryn Hill*. His performance with Hill at the 1999 Grammy Awards brought him back into the public eye.

Under a new contract with EMI records, Santana began working on a very contemporary sounding album, with guest appearances by some the brightest musicians of the day. Completed in the spring of 1999, the astonishing *Supernatural* album would bring Santana acclaim and praise that far exceeded his early successes.

As a member of the Rock 'n' Roll Hall of Fame, Santana has ensured himself of an honored place in popular music history.

A more peaceful Santana was able to appreciate his successes, his family, and his commitment to helping others. In 1998, he formed the Milagro Foundation with his wife. *Milagro* means miracle, and the mission of their organization is to do wonderful things for children through music and art. The Milagro Foundation creates band programs in schools and provides musical instruments to children in low-income families. In September 2000, Santana and Brown Shoe Company announced a line of "Carlos" footwear that will feature 14 styles of men's and women's shoes, with a portion of the proceeds being donated to the Milagro Foundation.

After an exhilarating and active year, Santana took six months off to concentrate on being a

Santana brings a unique enthusiasm and depth of emotion to his playing, helping him bring Latin-influenced music to audiences around the world.

father and husband until May 2001. Santana's follow-up to *Supernatural* is scheduled for release in the fall of 2001. While he is not sure of the direction the new album will take, he does know what he wants his music to accomplish. "What I want to do with music is pinch people, to see that we all have a passport to some kind of success with our grace and energy."

When he looks back at his life, Santana sees a pattern taking shape in the events of his life, a "perfect melody" that plays even in the midst of the hardest times. Although he has finally achieved the greatest fame of his life, he no longer needs to continue to prove himself. "My job is done—I don't need to win one more award, because my victory is done," he told *Rolling Stone*. "For me, if there is a theme to this, it is a masterpiece of joy."

CHRONOLOGY

1947   Born in Autlán de Navarro, Mexico.

1955   Moves to Tijuana, Mexico.

1961   Moves to San Francisco, California, and forms first band.

1966   Forms Santana Band.

1968   Signs with Columbia Records.

1969   Releases first album, *Santana*, and plays Woodstock.

1972   Becomes disciple of Sri Chinmoy.

1973   Marries Deborah King.

1974   Santana's *Greatest Hits* released.

1981   Parts with Sri Chinmoy; son Salvador is born.

1985   Daughter Stella is born.

1988   Wins Grammy for Best Rock Instrumental

1990   Daughter Angelica is born.

1992   Signs with Polydor/PLG Records

1996   Receives *Billboard*'s Century Award.

1997   Inducted into Bay Area Music Awards Hall of Fame.

1998   Inducted to Rock 'n' Roll Hall of Fame and Hollywood Walk of Fame; establishes Milagro Foundation; signs with EMI Records.

1999   Plays at Woodstock Anniversary Festival; release of *Supernatural.*

2000   Wins 9 Grammies and 3 Latin Grammies; voted VH-I Man of Year.

DISCOGRAPHY

Santana Band

1969	*Santana* (Double Platinum)
1979	*Abraxas* (Quadruple Platinum)
1971	*Santana III* (Double Platinum)
1972	*Caravenserai* (Platinum)
1973	*Welcome* (Gold)
1974	*Greatest Hits* (Double Platinum) *Borboletta* (Gold)
1975	*Lotus*
1976	*Amigos* (Gold) *Festival* (Gold)
1977	*Moonflower* (Platinum)
1978	*Inner Secrets*
1979	*Marathon* (Gold)
1981	*Zebop!* (Gold)
1982	*Shango*
1985	*Beyond Appearances*
1987	*Freedom*
1988	*Viva Santana!*
1992	*Milagro*
1993	*Sacred Fire*
1995	*Dance of the Rainbow Serpent*
1997	*Live at the Fillmore '68*
1998	*Santana* (Reissue) *Abraxas* (Reissue) *Santana III* (Reissue)
1999	*Supernatural* (Triple Platinum)

Santana solo

1972   *Live Carlos Santana* (Platinum)

1973   *Love Devotion Surrender* (Gold Album)

1974   *Illuminations*

1979   *Oneness Silver Dreams Golden Reality*

1980   *The Swing of Delight*

1983   *Havana Moon*

1987   *Blues for Salvado*

1990   *Spirits Dancing in the Flesh*

Santana Guest Appearances

1968   "Sonny Boy Williamson" (*Mike Bloomfield and Al Kooper: The Live Adventures of*)

1971   "Pretty As You Feel" (Jefferson Airplane: *Bark*)

           "Papa John's Down Home Blues" (Papa John Creach: *Papa John Creach*)

           "Streets Dude", "Spanish Gypsy", "Little Mama" (Luis Gasca: *Luis Gasca*)

1973   "Los Caballos" and "Morning Worship" (Alice Coltrane: *Eternity*)

1974   "Silver Sword" (Flora Purim: *Stories to Tell*)

1976   "First Love" (Narada Michael Walden, *Garden of Love Light*)

1978   "Friendship" (John McLaughlin: *Electric Guitarist*)

           "Latin Lady" (Gato Barbieri: *Tropico*)

           "Fried Neckbones" and "Home Fries" (Giants: *Giants*)

1980   "Saturday Night" (Herbie Hancock: *Monster*)

           "You Can Have Me Any Time" (Boz Scaggs: *Middle Man*)

           "Samba Pa Ti"(José Feliciano: *Escenas de Amor*)

1982   "I'll Never Stop Lovin' You, Saved" (Leon Patillo: *I'll Never Stop Lovin' You*)

           "Straight to the Top" and "I Just Want to Be Your Brother" (Stanley Clarke: *Let Me Know You*)

           "Hannibal" and "Señor Clarlos" (McCoy Tyner: *Looking Out*)

1984	"Lost Inside Your Love" and "Nobody Loves You" (Jim Capaldi: *One Man Mission*)
1985	"Push" (Aretha Franklin: *Who's Zoomin' Who*) "Marianne" (Gregg Rolie: *Gregg Rolie*)
1986	"This Is This" and "Man With the Copper Fingers" (Weather Report: *This Is This*) "The Beat of My Drum", "Loyin Loyin", "Ife L'oju L'aiye", "Akiwowo Ensamble", "Se Eni a Fe L'Amo-Kere Kere", and "Ilere Ilere Ilere" (Babatunde Olatunji: *Dance to the Beat of My Drum*)
1987	"Fire at Night" and "Too Late" (Gregg Rolie: *Gringo*) "*Forever . . . for Tonight*"(Neville Brothers: *Uptown*)
1988	"Black Manhattan", "Kinesis", and "Behind the Sunday" (Clyde Criner: *Behind the Sun*) "Tombstone Blues"(Bob Dylan: *Real Live*)
1989	"The Beat of My Drum", "Loyin Loyin", "Ife L'oju L'aiye", "Akiwowo Ensamble", and "Se Eni a Fe L'Amo-Kere Kere" (Babatunde Olatunji: *Drums of Passion: The Beat*) "Human Revolution" (Terri Lyne Carrington: *Real Life Story*) "Oh Yah Yeh" and "Trying Again" (Ndugu Leon Chancler: *Old Friends, New Friends*) "Too Close for Comfort" and "Tough Job" (Bobby Womack: *Save the Children*)
1990	"Who Is He" and "Lift Me Up" (Tremaine Hawkins: *Live*) "Psalms" (Alex Acuna and The Unknowns: *Thinking of You*)
1991	"Yele n Na", "Nyananfin" and "N B I Fe" (Salif Keita: *Amen*) "Stripped Me Naked" (John Lee Hooker: *Mr. Lucky*) "Soumba" (Mory Kante: *Touma*)
1992	"Reaching Out 2 U", "Todos Bajo la Misma Luna", "Samba Pa (Ottmar Liebert: *Solo para Ti*) On Song: "Mountain City" (Blues Traveler: *On Tour Forever*) On Songs: "Sette Massgana", "Caught in the Middle" and "Ras Clatt Ridd'm" (Caribbean All Stars: *Paths to Greatness*)
1994	On Song: "The Healer" (John Lee Hooker: *The Healer*)

1995	"Full Moon" (Paolo Rustichelli: *Mystic Jazz*)
	"Chill Out" (John Lee Hooker: *Chill Out*)
	"Get Down" (Junior Wells: *Everybody's Gettin' Some*)
	"Spanish Castle Magic" (Jimi Hendrix Tribute: *In from the Storm*)
1996	"Naima" (Angelique Kidjo: *Fifa*)
	"Get On", "Rastafario" and "Vers le Soleil" (Paolo Rustichellie: *Mystic Man*)
	"Eyesight to the Blind" and "Why Does Love Have to Be So Sad" (Erip Clapton: *Crossroads 2*)
1997	"Virgen Morena" (El Tri: *Cuando Tu No Estas*)
1998	"To Zion" (Lauryn Hill: *The Miseducation of Lauryn Hill*)

FURTHER READING

Heath, Chris. "The Epic Life of Carlos Santana." *Rolling Stone Magazine*, March 16, 2000.

Krulik, Nancy. *Pop Goes Latin!* New York: Putnam Publishing Group, 1999.

Leng, Simon. *Soul Sacrifice: The Santana Story.* London: SAF Publishing, 1998.

Shapiro, Marc. *Back on Top: Carlos Santana.* New York: St. Martin's Press, 2000.

INDEX

ABOUT THE AUTHOR

HENNA REMSTEIN is a communications professional and freelance writer in Philadelphia, Pennsylvania. She has written two other Chelsea House biographies, *Barbara Walters* and *William Tecumseh Sherman*, and contributed to several volumes of Chelsea House's Literary Criticism Series, including Asian-American Women Writers and Henrik Ibsen. She holds a B.A. in English from Temple University and an M.A. in Writing, Literature and Publishing from Emerson College.